TIME MANAGEMENT SECRETS

1.

'Time is the scarcest resource of the manager: if it is not managed, nothing else can be managed.'

Peter Drucker

This is the best quote to begin a journey of time management secrets as it emphasises its importance well. The first generation of time management consisted of creating simple check-lists that were more of a kneejerk reaction to situations. The 2nd generation used calendars and planning tools, which involved pro-active thinking. The 3rd generation of time management was about entering personal goals based on values into the planning. And the 4th generation was all about managing ourselves more than managing time. The current 5th generation is about managing electronic dependence.

I believe there is a short-cut through all of the above which leads to the greatest secret of all, and is covered in the following pages.

2.

'ONE OF THE SYMPTOMS OF AN APPROACHING NERVOUS BREAKDOWN IS THE BELIEF THAT ONE'S WORK IS TERRIBLY IMPORTANT.'

BERTRAND RUSSELL

Bertrand Russell is one of my favourite philosophers and I used this quote in my book on 'Getting Promoted', but it also has a powerful message for time management too: delegate whenever possible. Taking on more work will not necessarily impress the boss: a good time manager, if working in a team will divide up the work so he or she contributes a fair share, but avoids doing other people's work for them.

Time Management Secrets. David Hirst

3.

*'Take care of the minutes and
the hours will take care of
themselves.'*

Lord Chesterfield

This quote is a variation of 'Manage the pennies and the pounds will manage themselves', but is beautifully adapted to time management. It is often the case that people exclaim "Where did the time go!" And what they fail to notice is that while they think they are managing time in hours or even larger chunks, they fail to be productive in the minutes, so before they know it another hour or day has passed them by.

Manage time in minutes because they are the building blocks of wasted time.

Time Management Secrets. David Hirst

4.

'Nae man can tether time or tide.'

Robert Burns

While we may not be able to tether time, we can and should make the most of what is given to us. To begin, add the following: 21 (3 hours a day x 7 for eating, entertainment and leisure) + 45 (an average 40-hour contract week + commuting time) + 7 (1 hour a day for miscellaneous activities) + 56 (8 hours sleep a day x 7, although most people survive on less). You can vary these figures slightly to adjust to your particular circumstances. Now deduct this figure from 168 (the number of hours in a week) and you'll be left with a fairly accurate figure of the time you waste in a week: in this case thirty-nine hours.

This realisation is necessary to understand just how much time we have to invest in and do something with.

5.

'I don't think of the past. The only thing that matters is the everlasting present.'

Somerset Maugham

You can't change the past, so why worry about it? The present is crucial because it determines the future. If you can accept that you are in the position you are today because of the choices you made in the past, then you can shape your future by the decisions and choices you make today. And the luxury of the everlasting present is that you have the chance to influence the future every day.

Time Management Secrets. David Hirst

6.

'You delay, but time will not.'

Benjamin Franklin

Some people seem to think that as soon as they slow down with what they're doing, time will too. But it just doesn't work that way. And this is one of the biggest problems: procrastination. Especially on the small things. Putting things off merely delays the inevitable, so the best advice is to start the task as soon as possible, because the sooner you start, the sooner you finish. Everything looks daunting at the beginning, but as you make your way through the task, you will see that the value of time changes. It will often help to provide answers which weren't there in the beginning.

Time Management Secrets. David Hirst

7.

'Everything requires time. It is the only truly universal condition. All work takes place in time and uses up time. Yet most people take for granted this unique, irreplaceable, and necessary resource. Nothing else, perhaps, distinguishes effective executives as much as their tender loving care of time.'

Peter Drucker

I wonder how many of you reading this actually treat time with the respect and care that Peter Drucker mentions. In other words, how many of you use planning tools to map out what you intend to do with this precious resource? Simply put, we all assume that we will wake up tomorrow the same as we woke up today, and that is not always the case. We age, we get older and we change our attitudes to life, and before we know it, we start to wish we had done more when we were younger. The good news is that it's never too late to start planning your time.

Time Management Secrets. David Hirst

8.

'The bad news is time flies. The good news is you're the pilot.'

Michael Altshuler

I love this quote as it highlights that we can manage time by managing ourselves. And another recommendation for you to manage time more efficiently is to start making a to-do list of the three most *important* things you need to complete tomorrow. Now add one thing which 'Sharpens the saw' – something which is an investment in yourself. Do this every day and after a short while you will have started to achieve more in the time available.

Time Management Secrets. David Hirst

9.

'*All the flowers of all of the tomorrows are in the seeds of today.*'

Chinese Proverb

From your list of 101 things you wish to achieve before you breathe your last breath, you need to choose one – and I recommend selecting one that you can complete fairly quickly – and then make a start on completing it. Taking the first step is the most difficult, but when you do there is more of a commitment to finishing it and therefore enjoy its rewards. It also motivates you to take on the other challenges on the list. It all begins with the first step.

Time Management Secrets. David Hirst

10.

'*Nothing is ours except time.*'

Johann Goethe

I f time is all that we have, then one of the best ways of making the most of it is to do something productive. Rather than immediately turning on the TV when you arrive home, or go through your social media (again), plan to do something else such as read a book, participate in a sport or club activity, share an evening with friends, or just have an early night once in a while to feel refreshed and invigorated in the morning.

Time Management Secrets. David Hirst

11.

*'Things which matter most must never be at
the mercy of the things which matter least.'*

Johann Goethe

Another excellent tip for getting the most from the time available is to identify what the most important things are in your life. Write them here:

-

-

-

And then identify how much time you spend attending to them. How effective are you in keeping these things *first in your life*? Most people will admit that they do not spend as much time as they'd like with these important things. Why? Because they always put them off to a later date. So:

Step 1: Identify. Step 2: Assign – plan a set time.
Step 3: Act.

12.

'He who gains time gains everything.'

Benjamin Disraeli

ne very effective way of gaining time is to take control of your email inbox.

1. Immediately answer any emails that can be replied to quickly

2. Keep flowery writing to a minimum; write briefly, clearly and use simple words, phrases and sentences that you would say to the person's face.

3. Delete any emails that you haven't replied to after a month or archive them for reference later if you are sure you will need them.

Keep the clutter out of your inbox.

Time Management Secrets. David Hirst

13.

'Take a rest. A field that has rested yields a beautiful crop.'

Ovid

Although it may sound like an anathema to the young or even the young at heart, going to bed at a fairly regular time and early enough to ensure a good night's sleep is one of the most important time management secrets. Likewise, getting up early allows you to achieve more in the day. Conversely, staying awake longer does not guarantee greater productivity as the mind is not functioning optimally.

The well-proven English idiom *'Early to bed, early to rise, makes a man healthy, wealthy and wise.'* has been around for a long time.

Time Management Secrets. David Hirst

14.

'The worst days of those who enjoy what they do are better than the best days of those who don't.'

Jim Rohn

As we learn how precious time is, we should spend it (or invest in it) more wisely. So, have a look at your life and your list of 100 things to do (see secret # 7) and then decide if you are on the right path to having an enjoyable life. Consider that you may be happier if you take the measured risk of opening the newspaper and checking the job vacancies. Or even consider writing to that company which you admire, to see if they are planning any new posts in the future.

Time Management Secrets. David Hirst

15.

***'Even if you're on the right track, you'll get
run over if you just sit there.'***

Will Rogers

This quote reminds me of another time management secret: always keep your 'to-do list' in front of you as a reminder. Also, make a point of moving it to a different place every now and again (still in front of you though), as after a while it blends into the background scenery where you no longer notice it. Keep it relevant and keep it at the forefront of your thoughts.

Time Management Secrets. David Hirst

16.

'The cost of a thing is the amount of what I call life which is required to be exchanged for it, immediately or in the long run.'

Henry David Thoreau

Everything you do should have purpose otherwise the cost of doing whatever it is becomes too great. And too much time is wasted on the distractions that 'pop into your mind' as you are trying to complete another major or important task. Therefore, an excellent time management secret is to keep a digression log i.e. a record of when you suddenly remember to do something or check something out. Once you write down whatever it is that you remember, you can comfortably get back to your main task and not waste any brain power/space on trying to remember other things not related to the main task at hand.

Time Management Secrets. David Hirst

17.

'Live each day as if it be your last.'

Marcus Aurelius

In the days of gladiators or samurai warriors, each day was a blessing as they really didn't know if it was their last. Our lives may not be like this, but the message is still relevant: make sure you do something every day to ensure you move closer towards crossing something off your 'to-do' list or your 100 things you wish to achieve in your life. And make sure that whatever you do brings a smile you your life, because it really is too short.

Time Management Secrets. David Hirst

18.

'He does not seem to me to be a free man who does not sometimes do nothing.'

Cicero

Nothing time, daydreaming time, or (more precisely) thinking time is important. In fact, I would say it's crucial to successful self-management and therefore time management. For that reason, plan time to just think. Let your mind wander wherever it wants. This is the time when ideas form and life takes on new meaning. Write the ideas down – as you are likely to forget them if you don't – and then reflect on them to see if they offer a new insight to what you are doing and where you are going with your life.

Time Management Secrets. David Hirst

19.

'There is no one so old as to not think they may live a day longer.'

Cicero

We all assume that we will wake up tomorrow, but unfortunately many of us don't. Similarly, we all assume that we will be in the same physical and mental condition tomorrow as we are today. And this is also false. We get older and things change, often not noticeably until the difference is significant, and then it may be too late to achieve some of your dreams. Therefore, start your planning and goal setting today; act and then start crossing things off your lists.

Time Management Secrets. David Hirst

20.

'The time you enjoy wasting is not wasted time.'

Bertrand Russell

A lthough this quote may initially appear as a contradiction to many of the previous quotes, I would argue that it supports a little-known time management secret which is this: listen to music, have fun, do things that make you laugh as they make a big contribution to your overall health. And without good health you will function less efficiently than otherwise, which, in turn, will use up more of your time to get the same task done. Look after your health first: your time management will be better for it.

Time Management Secrets. David Hirst

21.

"There is no use trying", said Alice; "one can't believe impossible things".

"I dare say you haven't had much practice", said the Queen. "When I was your age, I always did it for half an hour a day. Why, sometimes I've believed as many as six impossible things before breakfast."

Lewis Carroll

For a lot of people, maintaining a clutter-free workstation seems impossible. As soon as someone forces them to tidy up, the clutter starts reappearing. The ironic thing is that if you ask these people about the mess, they usually reply that they have a place for everything and they know where this place is. However, there are two things wrong with this: the first is that trying to remember where it all is takes up a lot of processing power which could be used to better effect on main tasks. And second, there will inevitably come a time when they confuse the place they left something and have to search through piles of material to find it again. A clutter-free workstation is only impossible if there is no will to keep it that way.

Time Management Secrets. David Hirst

22.

'Start by doing what's necessary, then what's possible, and suddenly you are doing the impossible.'

St Francis of Assisi

The key message in this quote is in the first word: start. Procrastination is the killer of so many good ideas. Thinking about starting is arguably the most heinous crime in time management. Thinking is not doing. Planning is different as this leads to focus and efficiency, but merely thinking about starting something which has already been planned is criminal. As one sports manufacturer says 'Just Do It'.

Time Management Secrets. David Hirst

23.

*'A man who dares to waste one hour of life
has not discovered the value of life.'*

Charles Darwin

It is one of life's great ironies that people who really live life, appreciate every minute of it. Conversely, those who do very little, achieve very little and complain a lot. These people do not appreciate life until they near the end of it, and then it's too late. Try to ensure that you cross at least 3 things off from your 100 things to do list a year. See this as essential as food and water, for it is true nourishment for the soul.

Time Management Secrets. David Hirst

24.

*'If you want to make good use of your time,
you've got to know what's most important
and then give it all you've got.'*

Lee Iacocca

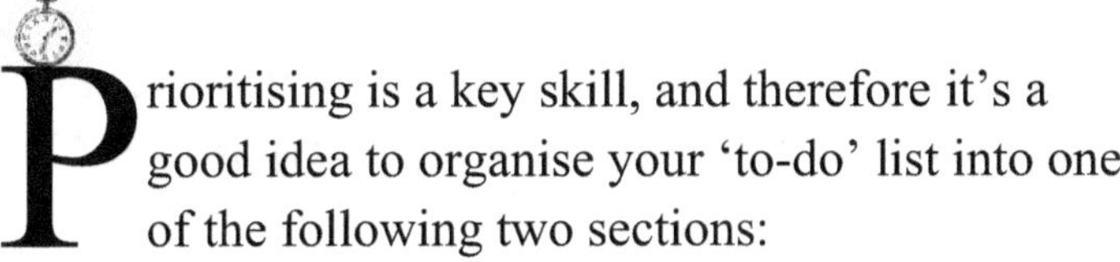

Prioritising is a key skill, and therefore it's a good idea to organise your 'to-do' list into one of the following two sections:

1. Important and Urgent
2. Important but not urgent.

Anything else is not important, so why are you considering doing it? Bear in mind fun things that are not related are also important, but probably not urgent. However, having fun **is** tremendously important.

Time Management Secrets. David Hirst

25.

*'It's not enough to be busy, so are the ants.
The question is, what are we busy about?'*

Henry David Thoreau

One of the main secrets of time management is to identify what your key purpose is at work. This is usually found in your job description and supported by your job plan. Time is squandered when people focus on doing tasks that they are not supposed to do or not required to do. These tasks may be fun or interesting, but they take you away from your main purpose. In other words, do plenty of what you are supposed to do and you will achieve a lot more in a shorter space of time.

Time Management Secrets. David Hirst

26.

'One cannot manage too many affairs: like pumpkins in the water, one pops up while you try to hold down the other.'

Chinese Proverb

Multi-tasking has been clearly proven to be less effective than single-focussed task completion. It takes time to re-focus on each occasion you shift from task to task. In fact, the more tasks you take on at one time, the longer it will take to achieve all of them compared with the sum of doing them all separately. Focus on one thing at a time.

Time Management Secrets. David Hirst

27.

'Never let yesterday use up today.'

Richard Nelson

There's no point in dwelling in the past as you simply can't change it. You can affect the future, but the past is over. We can learn from past mistakes and remember not to make them again, but always have your focus clearly in the present to affect the future. Mistakes happen, so don't let them affect the time you have to engineer a wonderful future.

Time Management Secrets. David Hirst

28.

'You cannot do a kindness too soon, for you never know how soon it will be too late.'

Ralph Waldo Emerson

We cannot know exactly how long our lives or the lives of our family and friends will be. We can hazard a guess based on our family history, but it could be wildly off, especially as we never know when an accident may come our way. Doing a kindness is an important event: it can have profound consequences. Therefore, never leave doing a kindness until tomorrow, as tomorrow is not a guaranteed thing. This will leave you with no regrets to think about and take up your time.

Time Management Secrets. David Hirst

29.

‘He who knows most grieves most for wasted time.’

Dante

This is probably why the older generation get frustrated with younger people hanging around doing very little, or why they criticise youth for not studying harder. The truth is that they probably did the same thing when they were the same age, but now that they're older they value time more as they can see what they have left being eroded every day. But the quote holds most true for those people who have experienced life and enjoyed what it has to offer. For these people, any wasted time in their early lives is grieved for.

Time Management Secrets. David Hirst

30.

'Make use of time, let not advantage slip.'

William Shakespeare

One of the best places to start making use of your time is with the amount you spend on social media and the Web. One of the easiest time management secrets to follow is to allocate a specific time every day for internet use. When this time is can vary, but ensure the **amount** you spend is strictly monitored. You may be surprised how much time goes by this way without really achieving very much.

Time Management Secrets. David Hirst

31.

'One worthwhile task carried to a successful conclusion is worth half-a-hundred half-finished tasks.'

Malcolm S. Forbes

There is a wonderful sense of worth and self-accomplishment when you can cross something off your to-do list. It just feels really good. It feels so good that it often becomes the motivating factor for the next task.

Time Management Secrets. David Hirst

32.

'If it's important, just do it.'

David Hirst

Having looked extensively at the research on time management and read widely on the subject, I feel very confident to say that this is the greatest secret of all. You can theorise until forever, but it nicely summarises everything I've read. And the reason I see it as the most important is that throughout my training programmes there is one common crime: people talk about doing things – great things – but that's usually as far as it ever gets. If it's important, just do it.

Time Management Secrets. David Hirst

33.

'A day may sink or save a realm'

Lord Alfred Tennyson

There are 3 important things to remember with the time you have in a day:

1. Be realistic with your 'to do' lists: generally, people are too ambitious with what they can achieve in a day.

2. What you do each day has a massive significance for your future life.

3. Generally, people underestimate how much they can achieve in a decade, because they fail to see how many days they have to work with.

Time Management Secrets. David Hirst

34.

'He who lets time rule him will live the life of a slave.'

John Arthorne

No-one wants to be a slave to time and one way to avoid this is to monitor the speed at which you do things. Do you slow down to an almost zero when the task becomes boring? Maintain a steady pace infused with regular doses of enthusiasm. If you have no enthusiasm for what you are doing then you have 2 choices: do something else; or do it faster so you can finish faster and then do something more enjoyable.

Time Management Secrets. David Hirst

35.

'In truth, people can generally make time for what they choose to do; it is not really the time but the will that is lacking.'

Sir John Lubbock

The reality is that we could all plan more effectively if we chose to. We also have no difficulty prioritising items, and we can usually organise those priorities well. But the main issue with all of these is the will to do so. At the root of all time management problems is the inability to discipline ourselves effectively. When you say you'll meet someone at a particular time, mean it. Be strict with organising yourself and time will obediently follow.

Time Management Secrets. David Hirst

36.

'The surest way to be late is to have plenty of time.'

Leo Kennedy

When a lot of time seems available, people seem to waste even more of it until they get to 'the last minute' when they become late for deadlines. A key cause of this is a lack of planning. There is rarely plenty of time, but if you find you have time on your hands because of a task you have completed faster than anticipated, then this is an excellent opportunity to continue developing checklists, to-do lists and prioritise tasks. Time spent planning is never wasted provided it leads to action.

Time Management Secrets. David Hirst

37.

*'Time has no meaning in itself unless we
choose to give it significance.'*

Leo Buscaglia

Whatever job you do; whatever occupation you have; you should always ask yourself one fundamental question: Why am I doing this? This question should help you understand the significance of doing the task. If there is an unsatisfactory answer, then you should really consider asking a few follow-up questions such as 'What would I be happier doing with my time?' or 'What other ways are there for me to earn a living, but enjoy doing the job more?' If you are spending 8 or more hours a day doing something that has no significance for you, then it's time to re-evaluate what you do and why you're doing it.

Time Management Secrets. David Hirst

38.

'We must use time as a tool, not as a crutch.'

John F. Kennedy

Absolutely! And one way to use time as a tool is to create mini-blueprints for more complex process tasks. In other words, to help you save juggling many different ideas and tasks at any one time, and to save processing power, you can create check lists which help ensure you have completed every step of the task to its completion. This will save you time in the long run.

Time Management Secrets. David Hirst

39.

'And thus the whirligig of time brings in his revenges.'

William Shakespeare

Time in this quote is likened to a merry-go-round which spins giddily around the individual. Time has its revenge if you do not invest in it wisely. The revenge will come in the form of regret, and once established, the regret can last as long as you live. The message in the quote therefore is to live life to the fullest, and make sure that every day you do something which brings a smile to your face and the face of others. Think of yours now!

Time Management Secrets. David Hirst

40.

'There's never enough time to do it right, but there's always enough time to do it over.'

Jack Bergman

This is surely one of those amazing facts of time. But why can't we get it right the first time and save ourselves the greater amount of wasted time that it takes to correct our mistakes? The answer lies in the idea that we can rush through things to save time, but with this approach the checking often gets put aside with the assumption that everything is fine. Hence the expression 'More haste, less speed'. Getting it right the first time may take a little longer if you apply thorough checks, but this is usually far quicker than having to correct mistakes later.

Time Management Secrets. David Hirst

41.

*'So much of our time is spent in preparation,
so much in routine, and so much in
retrospect, that the amount of each person's
genius is confined to a very few hours.'*

Ralph Waldo Emerson

With such little time left for genius, it's imperative that you use it to your best advantage. One of the best ways of doing this is to write down a personal 'mission statement' or a personal 'constitution', if you prefer that term instead. This should be a statement or statements which capture what you want out of life, the virtues you want to expand, and what you want to give. This forms the basis of goal setting and is the first step to planning. Above all, it allows you to inject more purpose into your life.

Time Management Secrets. David Hirst

42.

'We all run on two clocks. One is the outside clock, which ticks away our decades and brings us ceaselessly to the dry season. The other is the inside clock, where you are your own timekeeper and determine your own chronology, your own internal weather and your own rate of living. Sometimes the inner clock runs itself out long before the outer one, and you see a dead man going through the motions of living.'

Max Lerner

It is a very sad situation when a person gives up the enjoyment and fun of living. If you ever find yourself losing the fun in life, or seem to have very little to look forward to, an excellent way to change this is to shift perceptions. Although challenging, it is possible with a few poignant questions such as 'What is the one thing that if you began it today, would make a significant difference to your life in the future? Focus on this and act. The very fact of 'doing' will help you get back into really living again.

Time Management Secrets. David Hirst

43.

'Once you have mastered time, you will understand how true it is that most people overestimate what they can accomplish in a year – and underestimate what they can achieve in a decade.'

Anthony Robbins

I think it's also true to say that when it comes to
the to-do list for the day, people consistently
overestimate what they can accomplish because of
not building in emergencies. In any plan there must
always be time made for unexpected events. And if, by
some slim chance, that this time becomes available for
other things, then it's a bonus that you can invest in by
doing something productive such as thinking and
planning for the following day, or reading, or
something which makes you smile. People
overestimate what they can achieve in a year for
similar reasons. They underestimate what they can
achieve in a decade because it seems a long way away,
but the truth is that it isn't. A decade can pass quicker
than you think.

Time Management Secrets. David Hirst

44.

'I am only one, but still I am one. I cannot do everything, but still I can do something. I will not refuse to do the something I can do.'

Helen Keller

This is another key secret of effective time management: we are what we are as a result of our choices. If you are a product of your circumstances then you are ineffective. For the most part we choose to be late for meetings, appointments, training, social activities etc., because if it was important to us, we would make sure that we arrived on time. The vast majority of people arrive on time for work because they know that if they were late, they would lose their bonus, have their pay docked, or run the risk of losing their job. It becomes important.

Time Management Secrets. David Hirst

45.

'Clock watchers never seem to be having a good time.'

James C. Penney

People who are bored and unhappy with what they're doing note that the time drags.

Conversely, people who are motivated and cheerful about what they do say that time passes in an instant. This is why time just seems to disappear when you're having a good time with friends, but completing an arduous or meaningless task appears to take forever. Allocate specific and realistic amounts of time (deadlines) for each task and stick to them. Doing this will ensure you complete tasks faster than you would have otherwise, therefore saving time for other more enjoyable things.

46.

'Nothing is a waste of time if you use the experience wisely.'

Auguste Rodin

While we should aim to get things right the first time, we can't always be as successful as we can after several attempts. The main point here is that even if you are unsuccessful at something, the learning you get from the experience usually outweighs the time spent trying. This might appear like a contradiction. For example: trying to get each sentence perfect the first time when writing memos, reports and proposals, may actually take you longer than writing down what comes to mind and then editing later for correct grammar, punctuation, style etc. However, I would still class this as getting it right the first time i.e. before you press 'send'. If the boss sends it back with corrections then the learning begins. There's no failure; only feedback.

Time Management Secrets. David Hirst

47.

'The average American worker has fifty interruptions a day, of which seventy percent have nothing to do with work.'

W. Edwards Deming

I believe that the second greatest waste of time after procrastination is the theft of time by other people. It's often the case that if one person is having a bad day, they will have a chat with their colleague to calm down. And while keeping good working relationships is important, it must be put in the context of stolen time. You can always socialise after work or at a time that's *mutually* convenient. So, to save wasting time, stop stealing other people's. This includes asking yourself the crucial question: What if I didn't (send the email/message/CC unnecessarily, or bother them)?

Time Management Secrets. David Hirst

48.

'Setting goals is the first step in turning the invisible into the visible.'

Anthony Robbins

This quote applies to almost everything you do. It may be a cliché, but it is always worth reminding ourselves that very little gets done without planning. It helps avoid procrastination, as long as you apply realistic timelines, and gives a beginning, a journey, and a destiny. If you want anything in this life, you need to think how you're going to achieve it, because for sure it won't fall in your lap.

Time Management Secrets. David Hirst

49.

'A wise person does at once, what a fool does at last. Both do the same thing; only at different times.'

Baltasar Gracian

This is my favourite quote about how procrastination eats away at your time. We all have the same number of hours in the day, but some people use them to carve out their niche in the world and design their own success. Others are more reactive and put off the tasks they know they will eventually have to complete anyway. Choose success and don't delay.

Time Management Secrets. David Hirst

50.

'Don't say you don't have enough time. You have exactly the same number of hours per day that were given to Helen Keller, Pasteur, Michelangelo, Mother Teresa, Leonardo da Vinci, Thomas Jefferson and Albert Einstein.'

H. Jackson Brown

This is a nice follow-on from the previous quote regarding procrastination. An excellent way to spend a little time is to ask yourself what the difference is between these famous people (or anyone you admire), and yourself. You may find that the answer is surprisingly little. The difference could be dedication, enthusiasm, motivation, determination, perseverance and so on. The main issue here is that the qualities they possess are all part of being a great time manager. So, if you want to join the ranks of the rich and famous, your first step is to manage what you do with your time.

Time Management Secrets. David Hirst

51.

'Better three hours too soon, than one minute too late.'

William Shakespeare

That one minute too late could be the difference between success and failure. Being late is more of a choice than people believe. They make excuses such as the traffic was bad, there was an accident on the road, or train took longer than usual. And these are all likelihoods, but if the meeting is important, then you should also be able to plan for these possibilities. Being late usually means that there was something else of more importance that you decided to spend more time with. The question is therefore Did you prioritise effectively?

Time Management Secrets. David Hirst

52.

'It's not so much how busy you are, but why you are busy. The bee is praised. The mosquito is swatted.'

Mary O' Connor

being enthusiastic and working with haste are excellent qualities, but at the same time you need to keep asking yourself about the purpose of your speed. If the ultimate goal of what you're doing is a positive outcome for you and others, then it's time well spent. But if the goal is merely to kill time, then it's a waste. And it is a really bad waste if your thoughts and deeds are focussed on negative outcomes as a result of what Zig Ziglar terms 'stinkin' thinkin' i.e. your energy is directed towards hate, dislike and revenge. Being busy is fantastic, and a very productive use of time, provided there is a constructive result.

Time Management Secrets. David Hirst

53.

'I would rather be ashes than dust! I would rather that my spark should burn out in a brilliant blaze than it should be stifled by dry rot. I would rather be a superb meteor, every atom of me in magnificent glow, than a sleepy and permanent planet. The proper function of man is to live, not to exist. I shall not waste my days in trying to prolong them. I shall use my time.'

Jack London

One of the most powerful questions that I have ever been asked was 'What are you looking forward to doing in the future?' The reason it's so powerful is that if it's difficult to answer then you merely exist in the quagmire of life: you are not really living. Invest in time by thinking what you really want out of life, then you can start making the goal a reality by dividing it into short-, medium- and long-term sections, and then you have the makings of a plan.

Time Management Secrets. David Hirst

54.

'Time spent laughing is time spent with the gods.'

Japanese Proverb

To ensure you are living and not just existing, there should be at least one point in every day that you laugh. Laughter is a wonderful cure for many ailments; it is also an excellent motivator for better time management. If you spend time with tasks that encourage laughter, then it's time well invested. Life is about living, and to really live life you should enjoy every moment of it.

Time Management Secrets. David Hirst

55.

**_'Don't spend time beating on a wall, hoping
to transform it into a door.'_**

Dr. Laura Schlessinger

A lot of time is wasted by those who convince themselves that they can be something they are not. Dreams are so very important, but a good dose of reality is also necessary. Recognise what you can and can't do, then evaluate what is probable, then what is possible, and then what is desirable but currently impossible. All of them may be achievable, and try them all – even the impossible, but keep at least one foot grounded on the floor of reality because ultimately it will save you time. Moreover, after achieving several tasks which are probable, and perhaps a few that were only possible, you are in a much better position to challenge the so-called impossible.

Time Management Secrets, David Hirst

56.

'Waste no more time arguing what a good man should be, be one.'

Marcus Aurelius

This is another excellent quote pointing the finger at procrastination. Although planning is an excellent tool to help you achieve your goals, you can also over plan. This is when the plan becomes more the goal than the original reason for planning in the first place. So much time is wasted in meetings because there is so much talk and very little action. Rather, spend quite a lot of time thinking, a little time discussing, and most of the time doing.

Time Management Secrets. David Hirst

57.

'Time is the coin of your life. It is the only coin you have, and only you can determine how it will be spent. Be careful lest you let other people spend it for you.'

Carl Sandburg

ther people will happily steal your time if you let them. Try the following:

- Ask them why they have come to see you.
- Stand up when people come to see you – this hurries the other person to get to the point.
- If you need to see someone, go to them as it's easier to leave.
- Have the courage to ask them to come back later if you're in the middle of something.
- Be ruthless with time and gracious with people.

Time Management Secrets. David Hirst

58.

'Oh! Do not attack me with your watch. A watch is always too fast or too slow. I cannot be dictated to by a watch.'

Jane Austen

When you're having fun, time seems to go so fast. And when you are bored it seems to drag forever. However, one place that you should dictate time to is the phone. Try the following:

- Make your calls in blocks – don't let calls litter the day.
- Think about the call before you make it. Plan the outcome.
- Reduce idle chat, but always be polite and professional.
- Arrange to divert calls to a colleague when you are particularly busy, and offer to return the favour in future.

Time Management Secrets. David Hirst

59.

'Ordinary people think merely how they will spend their time; a man of intellect tries to use it.'

Schopenhauer

Use your intellect with your email and messaging Apps, since they are the most frequently used tools in business. Try the following:

- Never open SPAM however interesting it may look.
- Reserve personal emails and messages for lunchtime.
- Avoid 'reply all' unless absolutely necessary.
- Do you need to open all the attachments?
- De-clutter regularly, especially Apps.
- Think twice before replying and ask yourself if you really need to.
- Keep your answers to a minimum – sometimes 'Yes' or 'No thanks' is enough.

Time Management Secrets. David Hirst

60.

'There is never enough time, unless you're serving it.'

Malcolm S. Forbes

This is especially the case in meetings that your boss calls. He or she may have all the time in the world because they steal yours. Try the following:

- If you can, ask for an agenda with time margins.
- Ask if you can attend only the relevant parts.
- Minimise small talk and idle chat.
- Be prepared and turn up on time (even if the boss doesn't – catch up on some App messeges).
- Recommend that there should only be regular meetings if there is something new to add.

Time Management Secrets. David Hirst

61.

'Regret for wasted time is more wasted time.'

Mason Cooley

Avoid wasting more time by procrastinating and then regretting not starting the task earlier. To avoid procrastination, try the following:

- Start the day with the worst task – get it out of the way rather than have it in the back of your mind.
- Treat yourself to something you enjoy doing after completing unpleasant tasks.
- Set deadlines and stick to them.
- Avoid multi-tasking: do one thing at a time.

Time Management Secrets, David Hirst

62.

'Lost, yesterday, somewhere between sunrise and sunset, two golden hours, each set with sixty diamond minutes. No reward is offered for they are gone forever.'

Horace Mann

How much time have you wasted trying to find documents you were sure you had put on your desk? Instead of just an in tray and an out tray, try creating the following:

- Immediate answer tray
- Need more information tray
- Information only tray – read and pass on or bin
- Miscellaneous tray – stuff that doesn't fit into the other categories

Time Management Secrets. David Hirst

63.

'This is no time for ease and comfort. It is the time to dare and endure.'

Winston Churchill

Even when things are going well, really well, you should not 'rest on your laurels'. Although there will be the temptation to relax once you feel you have mastered time, do not ease your vigilance as it is a continual battle of wills. Stick to your plans; keep setting and achieving goals; and above all: just act.

Time Management Secrets. David Hirst

64.

***'The first hour of the morning is the rudder
of the day.'***

Henry Ward Beecher

This is the time that defines whether it will be a productive, achievement-filled day, or just another day. If every day is as important as all the previous quotes seem to suggest, then starting the day right is imperative. That also requires getting a good sleep the night before. This, in turn, requires a healthy diet and an active (exercise) lifestyle. So, starting the day well is quite a task, and if all fails then try and be as productive in the first hour because it sets your mental framework for the day.

Time Management Secrets. David Hirst

65.

'There is nothing more difficult to take in hand, more perilous to conduct, or more uncertain in its success, than to take the lead in the introduction of a new order of things.'
Niccolo Machiavelli

This is so true when it comes to stopping other people from stealing your time. As before, they will come to you for a shoulder to cry on, or to let off steam about something, or just to pass the time. And they will expect you to listen, just as before. However, if you are serious about using your time more efficiently you will have to become a little more Machiavellian about how you spend it. After all, it's yours, it's very precious because it can't be replaced, and it governs your success or failure. One place to be your new, more assertive you is with the interruptions you receive. If someone comes to see you, stand up; and if someone sits down near you then perch on the side of your desk. Be gracious, but use your body language to send the message that you have other things to do as well.

Time Management Secrets. David Hirst

66.

'When you are courting a nice girl, an hour seems like a second. When you sit on a red-hot cinder a second seems like an hour. That's relativity.'

Albert Einstein

This lovely humorous quote highlights the fact that the good times pass so quickly, while the time you spend doing something less enjoyable really drags. So, I recommend that every six months you take stock of what you are doing and why you are doing it. Try to look at your life from other people's perspectives to give yourself a more rounded and balanced picture. For example:

- What would your friend say about your life?
- What would your boss say about your life?
- What would someone you admire say about your life?
- What would your future self (in 10-30 years' time) say about your current life looking back at it?

If your introspection is unfavourable, consider what other possibilities there might be, and then act.

Time Management Secrets. David Hirst

67.

'How you spend your time is more important than how you spend your money. Money mistakes can be corrected, but time is gone forever.'

David Norris

Isn't it ironic that when you are young you have all these great ideas for what you would do if you had the money, and when you're older and you have the money, you have less inclination for doing all those wild things you used to think of doing. Don't worry too much about saving when you're young, go out and explore, have fun, and invest your time in developing your knowledge and skills. If you can, save a little, but saving should never be at the expense of wasting time.

Time Management Secrets. David Hirst

68.

'*Time and I against any two.*'

Baltasar Gracian

If you had all the time in the world you could achieve anything your heart desired. However, the reality is that we all have a limited amount of it, so we should make choices as to what we do with it. One of the best ways to invest your time is to invest in your own learning. Irrespective of how old you are, develop yourself. The younger you start, the greater the result, but it's never too late to start. Further, when you start seeing the results and enjoying the new life your efforts bring, you will want more. Then you will have truly conquered time.

Time Management Secrets. David Hirst

69.

'Don't let the fear of the time it will take to accomplish something stand in the way of your doing it. The time will pass anyway; we might just as well put that passing time to the best possible use.'

Earle Nightingale

Some dreams and goals look impossible before you start them because the end seems so far away. Then doubt starts to creep in to erode the dreams away into the corner of your mind labelled unachievable. But, as the quote suggests, the time you have will disappear anyway, so why not do something with it. One of the greatest personal crimes is not starting something you'd like to do because the end seems so far away. Because knowledge is increasing at an exponential rate, you may find that technology has made your impossible dreams possible if you begin your research. Start now.

Time Management Secrets. David Hirst

70.

'Living your life without a plan is like watching television with someone else holding the remote control.'

Peter Turla

S tart with an idea, a dream, an ambition, and then plan. The biggest mistakes people make when planning is that they try and fit all the personally important stuff into the planning mix last, which leaves very little time to achieve it. So, when you make a weekly or even a daily plan, make sure that the things that are important to you are put in first with all the other humdrum items fitting around them. Imagine the routine items are sand, the important things to you are rocks, and the bucket the amount of time you have. If you fill the bucket with sand first, it's very difficult to squash the rocks in afterwards. But if you put the rocks in first and pour the sand around them, then it's much easier to achieve a perfect fit.

Time Management Secrets, David Hirst

71.

'We can no more afford to spend major time on minor things than we can to spend minor time on major things.'

Jim Rohn

The biggest problem most people have with time management is not the lack of ability to prioritise, nor is it the lack of ability to organise these priorities, it's actually the lack of ability to act on these priorities that causes wasted time. Prioritisation is crucial to getting things done and acting on these priorities even more so. For that reason, identify the major (important) things in your life and act on them.

Time Management Secrets. David Hirst

72.

'I was part of that strange race of people aptly described as spending their lives doing things they detest to make money they don't want to buy things they don't need to impress people they dislike.'

Emile Henry Gauvreay

Unfortunately, there are a lot of people who dislike their jobs. They feel stuck in a rut that's hard to get out of, and the longer they stay, the harder it becomes to break free. If you are in this situation, cast your mind forward and try to see your life in 5 or even 10 years' time. If it looks the same, it follows that you should really start searching online for other openings. Another way of looking at this situation is to look ahead 3 – 5 years and envision a changed life; one that you enjoy. Try and picture the detail of it. After that, ask yourself what events would need to occur for you to enjoy that life. The answer you get is now the first step towards your new life.

73.

'Do not confuse motion and progress. A rocking horse keeps moving but does not make any progress.'

Alfred A. Montapert

If you find that you have no time in the day, you're always rushed off your feet, and you never seem to make any headway on your to-do list (assuming you actually have one), you really need to apply some of the time management secrets in this book. Take a look at how you spend your time. Keep a piece of paper with you and literally jot down everything – literally everything – you spend your time doing. At the end of the day, after you've gone home, have a look at the list of items and see if they were all important. If not, then there's something going wrong somewhere. Start with your daily and weekly plans.

Time Management Secrets. David Hirst

74.

'The key is in not spending time, but in investing it.'

Stephen Covey

What do you do with the time you have?
Most people I meet seem to waste a lot of
it on things which are unimportant (in the
greater scheme of things) such as checking their social
media every half an hour or even less, answering and
making calls that could wait, or creating impossible
lists with time frames that are simply unrealistic.

The answer to making the most of your time is to
ensure that you are investing in yourself – your
knowledge development – in the time available.

Time Management Secrets. David Hirst

75.

*'The memories you so fondly treasure are
being formed in the moments of today.'*

David Hirst

I'd like to add a quote of my own here to reinforce the preciousness of the time you have at the moment. To be a good time manager requires two fundamental things: an understanding of how valuable each day is to attaining your dreams; and also, an understanding of the greatest secret of time management which is this: if it's important, simply act on it. With this you will certainly achieve more in your life and have the chance to reach greatness. Now it's up to you.

Time Management Secrets. David Hirst